ALIVE I AM

Woman

NESI JORDAN

Contents

Dedication IV

"A lady talks to her father" 1

How Can I Reach You? 3

"We Are Women" 6

"The Misfit" 8

"Prayer Changes Things" 10

"The Day my spirit woke up" 11

"Papaya Girl" 12

"I've Heard a Word" 14

"I will Exalt you Lord" 18

"Replenishing" 20

Note 2 Self ! 21

"Pure Treasures" 23

Inspirational level 25

A Woman Who Sang the Blues 26

"Peels of the Spirit" 29

"Steer Clear of Forgiveness" 30

"Queen of Multi- Tasking" 33

"The Other Side of Fear" 36

The Power Of God's Word 40

What Belongs in the Light Will Shine 42

Dedication

The motivation behind this book was the Charisma of strong successful women that created a mark to rise up against their fears to share their Journey; With less anger and more power over what they thought controlled them. I've always admired testimonials that were transparent driven, the more that I sit and allow God to move through my spirit, he shows me through words what to do and say . Creativity is a must but being strong-willed is a challenge and I thank God for trusting me to move forward with this collaboration of women whom he created to conquer their storms and show God's Brilliance for the world to see. Thank you Lord! I am forever and truly grateful for all of the women in the world: I am My Sister's Keeper!

LOVE, NESI JORDAN

"A lady talks to her father"

"Record your brilliant moments not only in your mind but to inspire many of your dedication for peace."

L.K.J

Many thoughts run through my head putting my mind in focus. Hearing encouraging words from others, sometimes what my father has spoken. I'm changing my life on a steady path trying my best to forget the past, not saying it was bad only my father in heaven I could ever ask.

Emotionally things get hard but as I sing and pray I tend to let down my guard. There are so many things that I want to do, The gospel explosion wasn't the last that I'm going to do. I'm moving up the ladder and giving God all the praise and to have the little ones follow the pattern, that's how I was raised.

My heavenly father has added so many blessings in my life, I'm proud to say I'm somebody's wife. My wonderful husband is there by my side, my beautiful daughter I carried inside. I gained honesty, trust, love and forgiveness only if people knew but that's none of their business.

I had to learn with a blindfold over my eyes, the majority of my life my mom always told me, so it never was a surprise. I thank God each and every day for any and every miracle that he sends me each day.

I think of my heavenly Father, I pray to my heavenly father, I love my heavenly father because there's no other person all the time could be bothered.....But my Heavenly Father .

-CATHERINE

How Can I Reach You?

Father God how can I reach you? Why does it feel like I can't get a connection? Is it the signs or the glimpse of your vision that I watch almost fade away. You stopped and told me to do something with your power. Will you forgive me if I ask you again to guide and show me what I can't see? Father God will your goals for me change my life? Father will my faith begins to grow stronger …Father God will I stay in love with your words of encouragement longer? Father God how can I reach you? I extended my hand for you to pull me from this mess that I sunk into. My connection will always feel distant only because I don't know you, No more father! No more will I let my mind discourage what the enemy is doing to me I thank you for forgiving me and the plan you set for me….. Thank you for changing my life for the best I love you Lord.

−BRILLIANCE

"So glad to be blessed with the opportunity to be sensitive to the needs of others around me; May my actions communicate caring. I never want to become so preoccupied with what I want to say that I don't listen. Always stay humble but more so grateful for this thing called life."

–CILLA ANN

*Becoming a better you, Stand up and
do what's right for you!*

−SELFLESS

*My life purpose is to worship God with all my heart.
Fellowship more with my church family, other
Christians, get to know who God is and what he put
in my life with purpose. Learn to discern the will of
God. Glorify him! Give him all the praises. You need to
know that we can't do anything without the Lord.*

−THE BRIDE

"We Are Women"

We are women of courage
To stand when we need to.
We are women of integrity
To be honest with ourselves .
We are women of essence
To put the basic in our characters .
We are women of doubt
To put discernment into our lives.
We are women of fear
To not walk by ourselves in tough situations.
We are women of love
To welcome everyone, no matter what they have done.
We are women of long suffering to endure
all things whether good or bad.
Last but not least
We are women of Positivity
Not what others think
But what God made us to be.
In all Shapes, Sizes and Colors.

−DORIES

Then the Lord said to Moses "Go to pharaoh and say to him this is what the Lord says: let my people go so that they may worship me.

EXODUS 8:1

"The Misfit"

*Jesus said to them, "A prophet is not without
honor except in his own town, among his relatives
and in his own home."*

MARK 6:4

I was born a misfit, I didn't fit in with my family, and I didn't fit in with my peers. You see my maternal family was groomed in a cult. At a young age I questioned it and I was considered the black sheep, not by my mother, but other family members. All I can remember is just wanting to fit in, but something wouldn't allow me to, so I stood alone, or so I thought. My adolescent years were full of turmoil. I was picked on, talked about, and forced to fight. All because of the color of my skin, texture, and length of my hair. I never understood why my peers disliked me. I didn't know why they wanted to fight me for no apparent reason besides something I had no choice in or control over. This made me withdrawn, because in reality, I just didn't fit in.

Growing up for me was one crazy ride. I witnessed drug dealing, drug abuse, domestic violence, alcoholism, backstabbing, jealousy, hatred, and envy first hand in my family. I was a victim of child molestation, incest, bullying, domestic violence in my own relationship, teen motherhood, and giving birth to five children with three different fathers out of wedlock. I had three abortions. I experienced homelessness. I was addicted to marijuana, cigarettes, and sex. I suffered from depression and low self-esteem. Basically, I put myself through all that because I was different and I didn't know what to do about it. I tried to just fit in, but despite it all, I didn't. I was a misfit.

My self-discovery came when I truly began to search for Jesus. It's been a very long journey, but I'm here to share my story. In developing my relationship with my Savior, I discovered ME! Discovering myself allowed me to embrace my yesterdays and gave me the revelation that every misfit experience prepared me to fit into the Kingdom of God. I've realized that it's because of my past experiences that I am now able to reach back and pull up someone else. I wouldn't change my life for anything. I am who I am today because of it, and I like ME! Because of that, I can truly say that I am… "Alive I Am Woman".

-MINISTER ANGELA J.

"Prayer Changes Things"

"Seasoning things for a reason"

–CATHERINE

Follow the things that you know to grow wiser, Be able to be a decider. Challenges happen everyday and in many ways but Stay Firm in what you believe take the initiative to become better with your surroundings advocate for lost things. Fulfill your destiny become richer in your spirit, the truth is there. Stare off into space to withhold time ... open your heart for change make a point to go fulfill your inner thoughts.

AMEN

"The Day my spirit woke up"

There are many things that would symbolize our spirit to wake up. It only takes one day to realize what you have learned and chose to take responsibility for..... And that choice is you! I have grown in so many ways, let's start with the heart. My heart represents the kitchen of my life.

Where things grow and eat away by heat and the pressure begins to boil the temperature start to rise, glass get to breaking. We are the pages in a book and God is the cover, no matter how fast or slow we decide; God continues to keep us with a steady pace for that particular situation.

My famous phrases of the year was live life, continue to do what you love. My spirit brought a lot of people joy. My spirit brought me peace, the reason for peace is because the changes of my tone mentally and my growth physically.

Physically I had health issues that brought challenges to me mentally, that the race of my spirit continue to rush to do all things in order that patches up old habits of living bringing my new spirit up to date by burying and burning negative thoughts to hell.

-NESI J.

"Papaya Girl"

"Remember God produces year round"

-NESI J.

God is going to terminate the pain that has been done to you. Make believe answers won't grow your mind, the god honest truth is knowing you're worth as a woman. I will use papaya fruit as an example of a woman's worth. Papaya fruit is the healthiest fruit on earth it gives you healthy skin, it makes sure your digestive system is working properly and has high antioxidants.

I've researched the papaya fruit after the Holy Spirit giving it to me for the last page of this book alive I am woman. I didn't know quite where this word was going, I knew the message would be an amazing part of my testimony.

This fruit is very unique because I became more involved with the word papaya. papaya fruit was so deep into my spirit to the point I wanted to help impact the world daily and it doesn't bother me if it does not show the results right then because studying the meaning of papaya brought life to my heart and allowed God to translate to my mind that a papaya just isn't any fruit it's a form of what we all are and how God is our Creator and he created something good.

God is truly remarkable he has shown many ways of how the papaya can be used for a message of truth. Although a papaya has a slight seasonal peak in early summer and fall, papaya trees produce fruit year round.

That was so intriguing to me and I leave you with this; I feel we're never out of season even in our worst days, God picks the right time to show others how we've Grown with him, so if a papaya tree produces year round then God is the tree and he works with us year round as his fruit until we are ready when he chooses the season for us to come out and impact the world as women.

We are the best picked fruit, God formed purpose before we even knew it through our trials ,God still uses us to be great women as mothers, daughters, sisters, granddaughters, nieces, cousins and friends the most important is that we are Alive and We are still standing as women.

-NESI J.

"I've Heard a Word"

**Then God remembered Rachel; he listened
to her and enabled her to conceive.**

–GENESIS 30:22

My story starts in the year 1999. I was a young lady at the age of 21, I already had a toddler daughter. I just found out I was pregnant with my second child. As my belly began to grow, I felt new life beginning.

Monthly visits to the doctor's office for my prenatal care. The joy of being pregnant, blood work, prenatal vitamins, morning sickness, weight gain, weight loss, fatigue, change of appetite and excitement of the new baby's arrival.

The ultrasound day finally arrives what are we having (yes pure anticipation) it's a boy! Now it's time to go shopping, find a name and wait for baby.

Preparation for this bundle of joy couldn't have been more exciting, purchasing baby bottles, baby shoes, baby boy clothes, the baby shower, and everything blue. How much wonderful could this get?

The Baby shower was everything that a pregnant lady could ask for and more. This event was held at a restaurant it was private, I had many family and friends as my guests I received many, many gifts. My baby shower was very memorable and it was hard to ever forget. My baby shower was about two months before my due date.

Almost time for baby. A few weeks before my due date, I went to the hospital for a checkup approximately 38 weeks pregnant in the month of September. Doctors told me everything was fine with the baby and I didn't have long before my baby would be born. Oh how I didn't know that would be so true.

A few days later, meaning two days later my 2nd baby was born, STILLBORN. I named him Demario.

My daughter who was 4 years old at the time didn't understand what was going on and really was not comprehending why her baby brother had to go to heaven. She was a good girl and very helpful. I prayed with her to let her know things would be okay.

The following year 2000, as I try to grieve and compose myself from my heartbreak and loss from the previous year of my 1st born son I became pregnant again.

24 weeks or 6 months into the pregnancy I went into early labor, also in the month of September. Which is called preterm labor. The doctors couldn't stop my labor. My baby only survived a few minutes in this world it was a girl. I named her Kelly.

After the loss of Kelly I became really sick. I could barely walk from the basement to the main floor without feeling like I was going to pass out. I had lost a lot of blood. I was then hospitalized for about a week the doctors said my hemoglobin was very low. Generally a normal hemoglobin level for women range between 12.0-15.5 grams. My hemoglobin was a mere 2.0. I had to get emergency blood transfusion in order to survive.

I didn't want to have any more children after all of this heartbreak and agony but I prayed and guess what? Two years later in August 2002 I gave birth and was blessed with a healthy, beautiful baby girl, and two years after that in October 2004 I was blessed again with my last child a healthy, beautiful baby boy.

I am grateful for my children that I have. I have been blessed with my oldest daughter who is now 19 years old, she has now completed her first year at Michigan State University, my second daughter is 12 years old, she's an Artist, if not in no one else's eyes but mines that is fine, my youngest (my baby boy) he is 10 years old still loves to play and be a kid.

I also have angels in heaven. Gone but never forgotten. If anyone ever tell you that lightning never strikes twice in one place. Well they have never heard my story. I look at life like things happen for a reason.

These chain of events changed my life because now I understand the power of prayer, I don't dwell on a lot of things in life anymore. I like to keep it moving. I also understand when one door closes that means another door will soon open if you have faith. I use my strength to be strong for others when they are down and I try to let others know that they are not alone, especially when they tell me they have lost children at birth. Some people think since you have not had a lot of time with your child you can easily get over the loss of a stillborn, or miscarriage. That's not true, the bond between a mother and child is like a knotted long rope that can never ever be untangled forever.

Because I know where I came from, I know where I am going!

–MARKITA G.

*"To Remember where you have been by grace
and to know where you are headed by faith is
simply amazing; Glad the ears of my heart are
unstoppable, so I may hear the guidance."*

-BEYOND BLESSED

"I will Exalt you Lord"

**O Lord our Lord, how excellent is
thy name in all the earth!**

PSALM 8:9

I will exalt you Lord! For you rescued me! You refused to let my enemies triumph over me. (Proverbs 30:1) I have been angry in my spirit and heavy hearted. I have been angry and disappointed with people whom I trusted and held very near. I was distracted by those who I knew meant me no good. Searching and running… I've been bitter and just a mess.

I thank you Lord for pouring your Holy Spirit in me. Thank you for giving me the knowledge and know how to bow before you and place my stony, cold, broken heart in your hands. When my world fell apart, it seemed like forever that I wept for mercy face down on the floor, alone and broken. Going through that storm, you, Lord were protecting me.

I didn't understand then, but now it's clear. On the floor bowing before you, I was hidden under the shadow of your wings. Every tear I cried you collected. You poured your healing balm over my heart and made me WHOLE. Each day I prayed you drew me closer and said, be still for I AM the Lord your GOD! NO MAN will make you WHOLE, You are WHOLE in ME. In ME you will find the LOVE you seek!

God never said nor promised that would not go through trials in this life, but he promised that he would never leave us nor forsake us! As women we bear so much. We are mothers, teachers, wives, sisters, daughters, entrepreneurs, employees, employers, nurses, and the manager of our household. Sometimes without knowing it we get caught up in worshiping our husbands, children, jobs, and everything and everyone besides GOD.

Going through my storm, I was brought to a place of pure humbleness and unscripted WORSHIP of GOD. I fell in love with GOD. The life created outside of my marriage and abandonment almost destroyed me.

Selfishly I prayed to die. Never would I have thought this would have been me. BUT GOD! You see in this life I could have chosen to stay bitter, hurt and angry…BUT GOD. The MERCY and FAVOR that GOD extends to me, I must as a BELIEVER do the same. For I am NOT of THIS WORLD! I am a WOG…WOMAN of GOD!

I'm nowhere near perfect. I fall down, but I get back up! I try to spend time with GOD every day! HE HEALED ME. He made me WHOLE in HIM. For that I will be forever grateful! My eyes are on GOD. I know the path is straight and narrow, and seems so hard.

I promise all he wants is for you to reach out and take his hand. He will help you along the way and you will not walk alone. I ask that you fall in love with HIM too! For his love is a sweet spirit that is as cool as a summer breeze. He springs up fresh wells and his love and mercy endures!

I stand in the gap for all eyes to see and ears that hear. HEAVENLY FATHER I pray for COURAGE, DISCERNMENT, FAVOR, GRACE, WISDOM and MERCY.

I ask that you keep us focused LORD and DILIGENT in the work you have instilled in us. You walk with us daily and I ask that you bring PEACE over our lives, families, and our homes. Please fill our hearts with PEACE AND OVERFLOWING JOY!

You LORD said that your yoke is EASY and your burden is LIGHT. We humbly give you all of us… all of our cares and concerns… we give you our lives. Thank you JESUS for all that you have done and all you continue to do. Help us to be a light and a blessing to others. In JESUS' name AMEN!

Broken things can become BLESSED things IF you let GOD do the MENDING! Amen

Blessings,

–JOSLYN RENEE'

"Replenishing"

"Today is the day of fulfillment"

Replenishing my life! Feelings are more deeper than expressions. Expressions could surprise the one you love.

We all could hide our feelings and that expression can't just go to anyone. once that feeling is gone you have that right to replenish,God gives you that control before we know it, I want to learn how to replenish.

What I mean by that is what I want the Lord to allow me to replenish, the power Jesus has supplied with that right to be saved and secure with it.

-KAWAIN

Note 2 Self !

"Speak life over yourself even if you don't see it"

−AFFIRMATION

The woman that I've become is because of the wisdom that I've sought from God. Prudence is awesome I love the knowledge that flows, the understanding that follows and the wisdom that grows, beneath these walls are the ark of Safety, the fields of pain that burns within to change faithfully to please God.

I am a child of God, I am a brilliant mother, I am a woman of wisdom, I am a woman of fortune, I am a woman of wealth, I am an amazing writer, I am an awesome helpmate.

I am an inspirational speaker, I am a motivational speaker, I am a philanthropist by nature, I am an incredible lover, and I do have a peaceful home....

AMEN

"To Remember where you have been by grace and to know where you are headed by faith is simply amazing; Glad the ears of my heart are unstoppable, so I may hear the guidance."

BEYOND BLESSED

"Pure Treasures"

**He who finds a wife finds a good thing!
And obtains favor from the Lord.**

PROVERBS 18:22

I Am alive woman by Love, Grace, Peace, the Holy Spirit, and by Salvation, which is given freely to all.

I Am your song, your eyes, and the air you breathe.

I Am the one that loves you for you with no opinions, with no judgment or sound but, by my words of encouragement of Grace are you saved (Ephesians 2:8).

To save someone else.....

I should have told you it wasn't going to be easy

You were so innocent now you have gone through trials and tribulations.

The Source of Grace and Mercy that you did not deserve.

I was your peace and your protector when you had dark nights.

It is not of you but of me says the Lord.

I have guided you. I will send you your soul mate of truth and not a lie.

You will continue to cry that I'm your I Am!

That's the reason why you are the I Am Alive woman.

I Am Alive Woman of the Lord that humbles myself to help someone else but not to be taken advantage of but to do the Lord's will and try to follow his commandments.

It's not about me it's about we.

We can do it. Write! Plan! Do! (James 2:17)

Faith without works is dead.

I Thank Jesus who is the head of my life

and Nesi Jordan who is positive and encouraging for letting me be apart of her vision.

-MARLOW

Dear Marlow West,

I never thought I would be writing a letter of goodbye to one of my dear friends, business partner and little sister with an old soul of wisdom. I remember before I came to know you as my neighbor,I believe that you were a elderly woman that was consistent in her prayers....When I heard those prayers it blessed my spirit and encouraged me to get back to do more of praying in my household. Finally I met the woman behind the wall and was surprised to see a little woman with a powerful voice sitting on the porch with her little son Marlon sharing a hot dog selling flyer. That day we became close and started executing our goals...We had laughed,cried and prayed together, you will be truly missed for your forever Support, Holy Spirit led energy, Entrepreneurial mindset,Love and Patience for all people. I am truly grateful you had a chance to be a part of " Alive I am woman " before others saw it ...At least you knew it was going to be done. I love you my sister and your voice of support will forever ring in my heart in your last words for me..... Let's Get It Nesi Jordan!

Until We Meet Again,
Nesi

Inspirational level

Inspiration comes from God....Looking around your space of living, What do you see? How do you feel? What can come out of your emotions of your mind? What desires do you have to change?

-YOUR ANSWERS

A Woman Who Sang the Blues

He said to her," Daughter, your faith has healed you.
Go in peace and be freed from your suffering."

-MARK 5:34

A woman who sang the blues when she was sad. The blues weren't the only thing that flowed out of her mouth. It wasn't always about the blues. She spoke about her life and how she grew up from filthy rags to being on the way to riches. This woman sang about how she strained and struggled with different abuses: physical, mental, drinking, and addiction to prescription pills. This woman often spoke about being a prostitute but not getting paid. The men gave her what her mind and body craved. money wasn't the cost of her body but that addiction was what made her thrive.

The woman who sang the blues had to do what she could to survive, even if it was very unhealthy. The woman made up her mind to clear and erase the misery, addictions, pain, and hurt over the loss of her mother. Her mother spoke with her about change but the woman rarely wanted to listen. She used to wake up every morning with a hangover. She sometimes had bruises on her face from different male friends that used her temple to take out frustration. They didn't desire to help her.

Two months later the woman's mother passed away. She woke up sober and alone in her bed that morning. There were no bruises on her face that morning. She wasn't feening for any alcohol or prescription pills to get her high that morning. The woman who sang the blues took her shower ate breakfast, looked around her house, and started tearing down the yellowish color newspaper off the windows that had been there for two years.

The woman opened all her windows to let in some light. She stretched out her arms and sang a little tune her mother use to sing . The woman got some old rags out of the closet and start wiping down the walls, windows, and scrubbing the hardwood floor. As the woman scrubbed the floor, a little child appeared at the door. She seemed like she was lost. The child wanted to know if the woman had any eggs. The woman replied, "Yes, I do! Do you need some?"

The child said, "No".

"Why did you ask?"

"Because we are unequally yoked." The woman didn't understand.

The lost child asked, "Do you have any bread?"

The woman responded, "Yes, do you need some?"

"No, I don`t."

"So, why did you ask me?"

"It's better to not need it, than need it and not have it."

The woman looked puzzled. She said to the lost child, "What does that mean? I have bread and I eat it all the time. What are you talking about?"

The child took her hand, wiped the sweat from her eyebrow, and asked the woman, "Do you have any grape juice?"

The woman sighed. "Why? You're going to say you don't need it."

 The lost child says, "By any means no."

The woman said, "Of course I do. Why?"

"Because we're going to need it with our bread."

"I just ate breakfast."

"Not the same as I."

The woman replied, "What do you mean? I had sausage, waffles, and a bowl of buttered grits."

"Well we're going to eat again."

"Why are you picking with me? I'm trying to get myself together," the woman said in an irritated voice.

"I know, but you needed me to teach you the right food to start with first."

The woman looked confused. "What?"

"You started your day cleaning with your used rags. That's what we do when we are asking for a change. I pass by this house everyday. The windows are dusty. Light doesn't shine through. The door is always closed. Today I passed by and the windows were clear, light was shining, and the door wide open. I smelled disinfectant and floor polish. The first step was you wanted to clean. No one forced you. Next, you answered my questions and didn't get mad. Third, you have all the right things but didn't eat them yet. That's why I asked about the eggs. we can be equally yoked. You cleaned your home, which is your heart. You have bread. That's the body of your savior."

The woman asked, "Who?"

The lost child said, "Let me finish. You have grape juice and that represents the blood of our savior Jesus Christ. Now we can eat this and use your eggs to be equally yoked."

"I realize who you really are! My mother always talked about guardian angels."

"Yep, that's me. I'm in human form. I am a female because I knew you weren't strong enough. Men have used you but they can't abuse you any longer. I, the lost child, received a blessing, teaching you what's the right thing to eat."

The woman and the lost child sat on the clean floor. The woman poured the grape juice and broke the bread. and put the two eggs to cleanse my soul and never part from me.

The woman repeated after the lost child and she felt cleansed. The lost child smiled and said, "Now we can eat. This is what we call communion. This bread is the body of Christ. This juice is the blood Jesus shed for our sins and we do this in remembrance of him."

The woman and the lost child laughed and enjoyed their moment together. The lost child looked towards the light and said she had to leave. The woman asked when will she see her again. the lost child says you will always be on my route because you found the root to your situation and once you accepted the assignment you're forever in the vine.

—NESI J.

"Peels of the Spirit"

**"I will not leave you comfortless:
I will come to you."**

JOHN 14:18

Full of the spirit....Does anyone know what that means? It could be any spirit that you pick up without cleaning. Oh! There are many different spirits that are peeled from your day to day scar: Is it a spirit that abused you, hurt you, neglected you, loved you, lusted for you, cheated you, lied to you or even confused you?

The Holy Spirit will guide you mentally to break them down to help you bring peace around you; Does anyone know what that means? We're still trying to learn how to sense the spirit because we love to peel scars but when the Holy Spirit peels it, you don't want to Savor the feeling because the true reality unfolds the mask to forgive and move on.

My question to you: How long will you peel the scar and stop picking once it's healed? What are you going to do about it? Don't be afraid to ask yourself that question.

-KAWAIN

"Steer Clear of Forgiveness"

***Do nothing out of selfish ambition or vain conceit, but
in humility consider others better than yourselves.***

PHILLIPIANS 2:3

In Forgiveness I found out that it made me a better person. It gave me wisdom and the freedom to choose to be the woman I am today. I regained my courage and it renewed my spirit. It gave me a new release of life. I forgave from my heart, my mind, and my spirit. I was no longer the victim of unforgiveness, fear, and hatred. Instead I have become a more forgiving, compassionate, and loving person. It took me a long time to heal but I did. It was long before I let go and let God have his way.

Forgiveness cleaned my heart right where it needed to be. It gave me back my strength and power. It also encouraged me to live my life according to God's will and purpose, which enlightened and empowered me. I had the courage to know the difference, that the battle was the Lord's and not mine.

Forgiveness was a gift for me. I am so thankful God's grace kept me and I was obedient to Him. Forgiveness restored my spirit to love. It helped me to not be bitter and have resentment. In conclusion I had to forgive myself for not trusting God to heal my heart and soul. God has been so good to me. I know it was God leading and guiding me to become stronger than before and gave me the courage to let go of unforgiveness. I am loving my life and grateful to God for healing me. Forgiveness has made me the person I am today.

-KATRINA

*"And when the seven among four thousand,
how many baskets full of fragments took
ye up? And they said,"seven."*

MARK 8:20

"When you decide to make a change in some areas of your life. God will continue to do pruning if you forget about others feelings; Allow God to bring brilliance out of you. You have a purpose and God's plan is already written.... Shadows aren't seen as a real person. Step into the light!"

#TEAM NEWNESS

"Queen of Multi- Tasking"

*There is a time for everything, and a season
for every activity under the heavens:*

-ECCLESIASTES 3:1

New International Version

Patience is a virtue that we have but don't use as often as we should. We want what we want, when we want it. When it doesn't work out that way, we get filled with negative emotions such as disappointment, frustration, and/or anger. We have so many things going on in our lives. At times, it is too much. There is no way we can finish everything that we have committed to doing. We are often exhausted.

There is a time for everything but there isn't time for *everything*. As women, we have bought into the concept that we are supposed to be super women. We should be able to do everything. Our grandmothers, mothers, aunts, and female role models were able to do it all. Not only did they do it all but they made it seem easy. They didn't complain, they just got things done. We can take care of home, family, friends, work, and any other tasks that come our way.

There is time for everything but ourselves. Once we finish doing everything, the only thing we have time for is sleep and sometimes there isn't enough time to get the sleep we need. Our days are filled with activities. We get started early in the morning and keep going until late at night. The next day we do it again. Day after day. Week after week. We are queens of multi-tasking. We give pieces of ourselves to everyone.

Then one day we realize we aren't living. We are just alive. We love our families, friends, neighbors, jobs, etc. We were so busy doing everything for everybody, we forgot to love ourselves. We forgot to do something for ourselves.

It's time to put the "*a*" back into the sentence. There is *a* time for everything. It's also time to read the rest of the sentence. There is a time for everything *and a season for every activity under the heavens.* There is a season for every activity. We don't have to get it all done today, this week, or this month. Some things can wait for their season.

We can put some things to the side and make time for ourselves, our dreams, and our goals. Set aside time to focus on what you want. Figure out a way to make your dreams a reality. Decide when it's going to be your season. It's not too late. There is still time to make it happen.

–CANDACE

"So excited to have love embrace and give security, peace that floods my heart and gives me serenity ; Glad to be enjoying life as it unfolds, Timing is amazing!

BEYOND FAVOR

"The Other Side of Fear"

"Everything you want is on the other side of fear."

– JACK CANFIELD

I use to run when I came face to face with fear. Not the typical fear like standing up for oneself or confronting a bully on someone else's behalf. I seem to be quite good at that and could do it with ease... but there was this other type of fear. It would only appear when I attempted to do something positive to change my life and my family's life for the better. As long as I wasn't making any effort to improve myself I was fine. All I had to deal with was the normal day-to-day stresses, pressures, and responsibilities.

When I decide to get up and try again, go for a set goal, dream, or mostly when I would go back to school. I would get slammed, lied on, hit with back-to-back unexpected bills, kids acting up in school, or a child would get sick. Important paper work either needed to be renewed, approved, submitted. It would get rejected, lost, and for some reason I couldn't even get the email to work correctly to submit it. It was mind boggling!

I felt as though something or someone was trying to stop me from getting where I was attempting to go. I started to research and the first place I went was straight to the bible. This time I was determined to gain understanding, wisdom, and knowledge. I started to listen to successful people. Their stories of how they obtained success. I knew that there had to be a common thread, and there was. They all would come under so much pressure and unusual suffering when they would make up their minds to make a change for the betterment of themselves, their families and/or their communities. They would speak about how the closer they got, the worse the pressure became.

T.D Jakes compared it to giving birth. He said that "you have to give birth to your dreams and that the worse the pressure became... the closer you are to obtaining that dream." "Not to give-up and, just keep pushing." So as a woman gives birth to her child/children... the very minute she holds her baby/babies she forgets about the pain."

So I will go after my dream of starting my business for the umpteenth time. This time will be different, because this time, I won't give up! I've learned to understand the territory that I'm in. I appreciate the process of becoming successful. I am giving birth to my dreams. I can't wait to witness my accomplishments.

As the mother of three children, I can truly understand the process of giving birth. When I heard T.D Jakes speak those words, it truly helped me to understand the process and everything made sense. I have adjusted my mental, spiritual, and physical being to approach any and everything as though I'm giving birth. I nurture my dreams as though it's my child. I'm more patient. I understand the time it takes to incubate and I prepared myself for it's arrival.

-SHAREN

Impact 3 The beginning of my health season i thought was a crash and burn situation, never knowing what would happen next. I can tell you with all these unexpected stress balls thrown at my health....Let's just say every time I've gotten disappointed with the medical world. I have become very fluent with my body, many decisions are being made before I can even say anything. God is the note writer in my life or shall I say note taker....Every detail we may think we know, it never works out on our terms.

Our innocence comes back when we get that understanding to discern what God truly reveals to us. Many situations can be at a stand still waiting for the right time to support your viewing of each step. If there is an area of jealousy and just plain old nonsense that will bring forth a hinderance spirit. Some of the health support try their best to help get you well but every revelation ends differently. Bringing back the beginning it was a strong experience I went from a storm and conquered into a hurricane that brought an impact.... Impact means to strike with force; to pack firmly; to have an effect on.

As I start to pick up the pieces that's hard to figure out, it's really what the whole puzzle looks like when you're done, that get you thinking. Our puzzles are more like a never ending story until we leave this earth. My childhood puzzle ended when I became a teenager as a child I remember when I was ten years old my 32 year old uncle passed away from kidney failure, that was my maternal grandmother's oldest son. I remember my maternal grandmother taking care of him, My uncle was the one who taught me how to ride my bike and walked my little brother and I to elementary school when my granny couldn't.

My teenage puzzle ended when I became an adult I remember my friend from Junior High school he got shot in the back of the head only 15 years old surely at the wrong place at the wrong time. Another puzzle for adulthood that is still going but quite confusing, my mother's oldest and only sister passed away at the age of 52 she went into surgery for a liver transplant and never came out...Days after I found out I was pregnant with my second child, My family was so puzzled.

Another one of my adult puzzle pieces is my maternal grandfather he left this earth when I was 32 years old that was an impact situation I couldn't express, I still think to this day about losing my pa pa a lot of harbouring pain in my heart because how he passed, my family actually sat and watched him take his last breath. My Papa was 83 years old and you never would have thought his age because he was so youthful and worked like a champ, He was a grandparent that protected his family from struggles, and you didn't owe him a thing as long as he had it you got it. My granddad helped me get through tough patches in my life of 32 years....Papa gave his all for his children , grandchildren and greats.

I can go on and on with the stories about my grandfather, It's one particular memory I want to share and that's when i was around 4 or 5 years old my pa pa planted me a pear tree in my their backyard, that old pear tree grew bigger and wider to the point the pears were dropping everywhere in my granny's garden in the alley even in both of the next door neighbor's yard. My granny decided to cut the pear tree down, of course my papa didn't want to tell me that because it was his idea to plant it. I realize now it's about moments and it doesn't last long but be grateful and keep those great times with you for the times you're down or need a good laugh.

–NESI

The Power Of God's Word

So is my word that goes out from my mouth: It will not return to me empty but will accomplish what I desire and achieve the purpose for which I sent it.

(NIV) ISAIAH 55:11

In a world that's sin filled, sick and dying, we encounter many adversities. Sickness, unemployment, brokenness in our relationships and the spirit of division. God's word was intended as a guideline to follow to help us as believers to overcome. Jesus experienced many adversities but He overcame them. We as believers must know " **The Power Of God's Word**" by speaking, confessing, decreeing, declaring an lastly by walking in it. When we do all that I previously wrote about how we become **"VICTORIOUS"**. Victorious in our trials, in sickness, on our jobs and through weapons that have been formed but won't prosper. God is Almighty and Majestic which means His word has "Dunamis" power behind it. Our Father will not allow the things of this world overtake us but we must do our part. Pray, study, meditate and take Him at His word. How can we truly know the **"VICTORIOUS OF GOD'S WORD"** if we don't allow ourselves to experience it. In the bible many a times all Jesus had to do was speak God's word & it was so. He didn't have to be present. Remember, Faith is the substance of things hoped for, the evidence of things not seen.

Prayer: Father in the name of Jesus, thank you for your word. Thank you for the power of your word and what you send it forth to accomplish, be it healing, strength or even wisdom. Teach us to simply take you at your word and experience your word and its power... Shalom

ELDER LASONYA H.

What Belongs in the Light Will Shine

And he said unto her, Daughter, be of good comfort:
thy faith hath made thee whole; go in peace.

LUKE 8:48

I praise God for this moment! Every thought I put on paper I utilize every opportunity to share the brilliance of God. In October 2012 I almost died having my 4th son, My placenta was attached to the uterine wall and i almost bled out during a C-section. My youngest son was on 70% oxygen in the N.I.C.U, I thank God we are still here! In 2013 I was introduced to a young lady that spoke life into my situation; you would have thought it was all a bad dream but of course God has a plan for us all to follow, his purpose is truly remarkable. This young lady that is a Prophetess Spoke what the Holy Spirit laid on her heart and boy was I nervous. Prophetess spoke that my youngest son has a speech delay but he will have fluent speech and when he gets older he will be a powerful man of God in the ministry like Bishop T.d Jakes, she spoke that I will be at a cancer center but I didn't have cancer, Prophetess spoke also about me speaking and sharing my testimony and able to touch and spread awareness to help women all over the world. 2 years later all these things came to past except 1 only because my son was only 4 years old now 7 and doesn't know what ministering quite mean. I had an appointment with a hematologist at the U of M hospital cancer center and there was No cancer, my youngest son's speech is coming along and he can sing his heart out,I spoke at a women's tea and shared my testimony. In 2017 I became a part of a company that spreads women's health awareness all over the world and I feel so liberated! The greatest reward is being able to fulfill whatever the Lord's purpose is. GOD IS TRULY STUPENDOUS AT WHAT HE ALREADY KNOWS! I thank God for sending a true woman of God in my life to help Glorify God's mighty work.

ALIVE I AM WOMAN!!

NESI JORDAN

Cheers To You All!